NATIVITY STORY PICTURE BOOK

The Christmas Storybook

Andrea Clarke Pratt

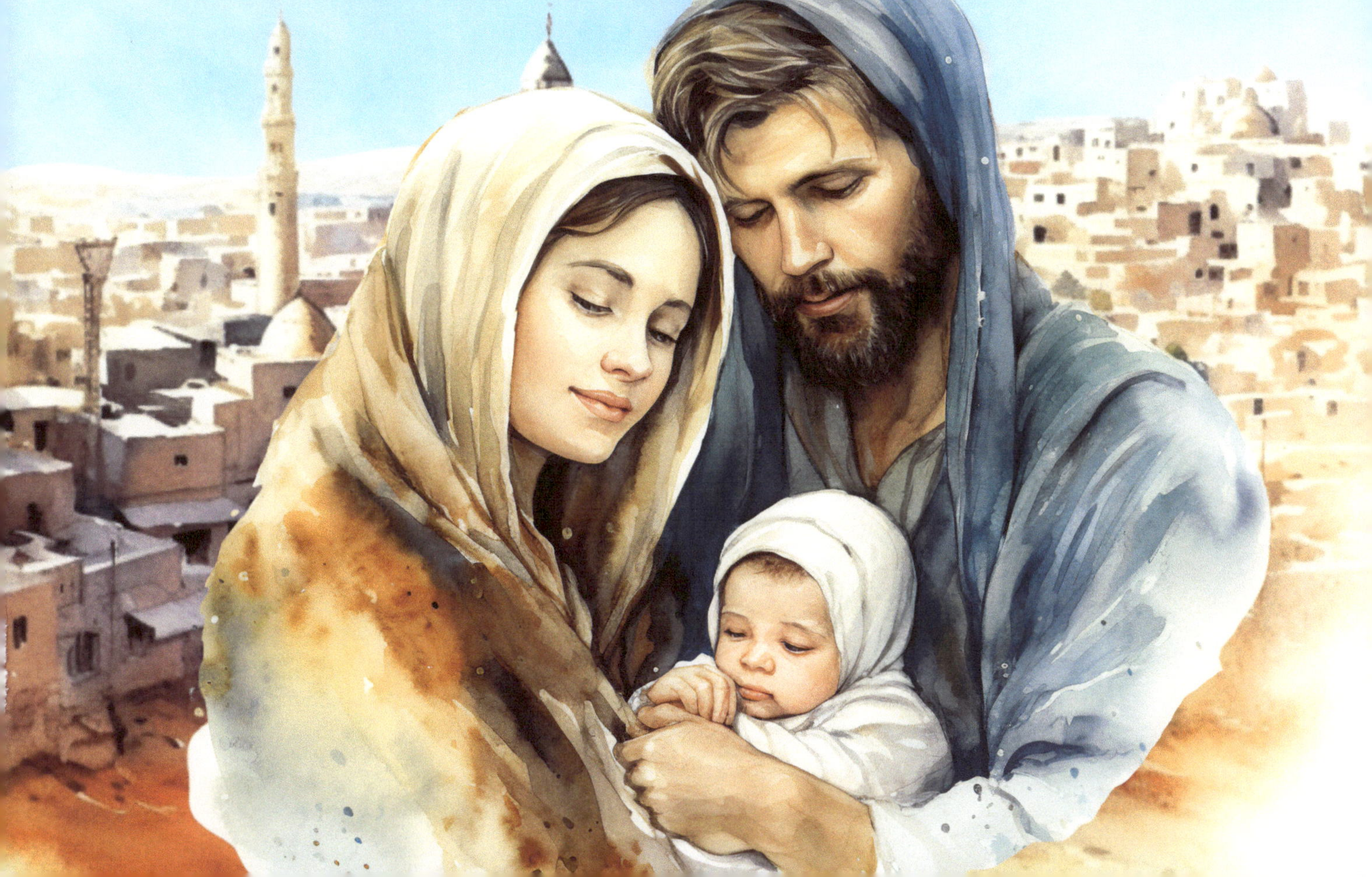

Copyright@2023. All rights reserved.
Andrea Clarke Pratt

This Book Belongs To

_____

_____

_____

From:

_____

_____

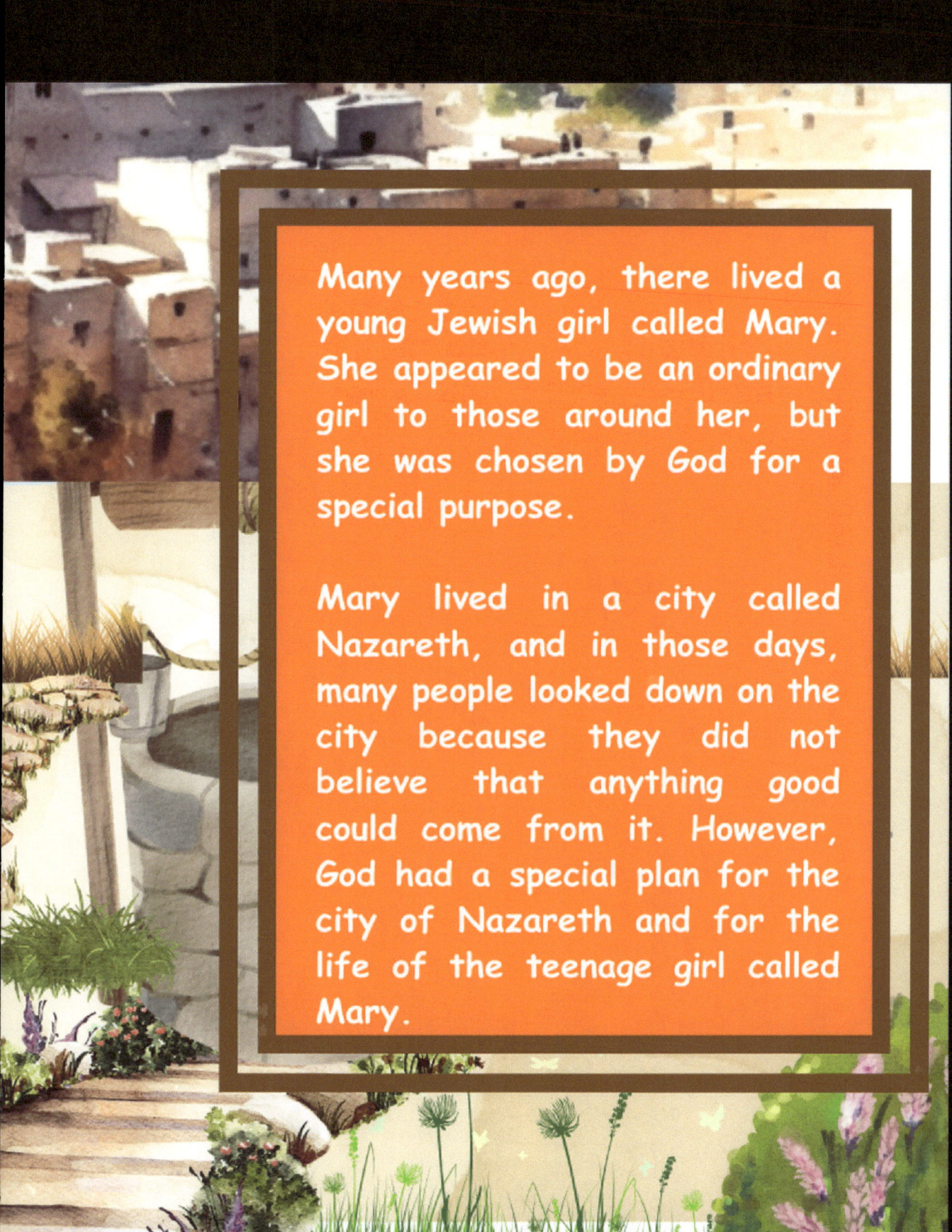

Many years ago, there lived a young Jewish girl called Mary. She appeared to be an ordinary girl to those around her, but she was chosen by God for a special purpose.

Mary lived in a city called Nazareth, and in those days, many people looked down on the city because they did not believe that anything good could come from it. However, God had a special plan for the city of Nazareth and for the life of the teenage girl called Mary.

In the past, God used the archangel Gabriel to make announcements and explain visions.

One day, God sent Gabriel to Mary with important news. Gabriel began by reassuring Mary that she should not be afraid.

He then went on to tell her that she was very precious to God and that she would give birth to a baby boy.

Gabriel told Mary that she was to name her son Jesus, which means Savior. Mary would not have known at the time that there would be great power in the name of Jesus and that even the devil would tremble at it.

The angel also said that Jesus would be great. Mary's son would rule over a kingdom that would never end.

Mary asked the angel how this would occur. She was still a virgin and was not yet married. She was only engaged to a man named Joseph at the time. However, the angel told her that the Holy Spirit would come, and God's power would overshadow her. Mary's son would, therefore, be the son of God.

Mary humbly told the angel that she was willing to do as God instructed. Gabriel then surprised her by telling her that her cousin, who was very old and could not bear children, was now pregnant. "For with God, nothing shall be impossible," said Gabriel.

Mary was engaged to a God-fearing man named Joseph, who was a carpenter by trade. Can you imagine how he must have felt when he learned that Mary was pregnant? They were unmarried, and he had not had sexual intercourse with her. He knew that he was not the baby's father.

Joseph was a compassionate man who cared for Mary, and because he was well aware of the awful things that could happen to her, he decided to end the marriage agreement secretly. It shows that he was a caring man who did not want her to be humiliated or put to death.

However, God sent his angel Gabriel to Joseph, and he appeared to Joseph at night in a dream. Gabriel told him that he should marry Mary and reassured him that she was indeed pregnant by the Holy Spirit. He also confirmed that the baby should be named Jesus, as he would save his people from their sins.

Joseph awoke from his dream and felt reassured to marry Mary.

He trusted God and decided to obey the instructions that the angel had delivered to him. It is important to obey God's instructions because God loves us and has our best interests at heart.

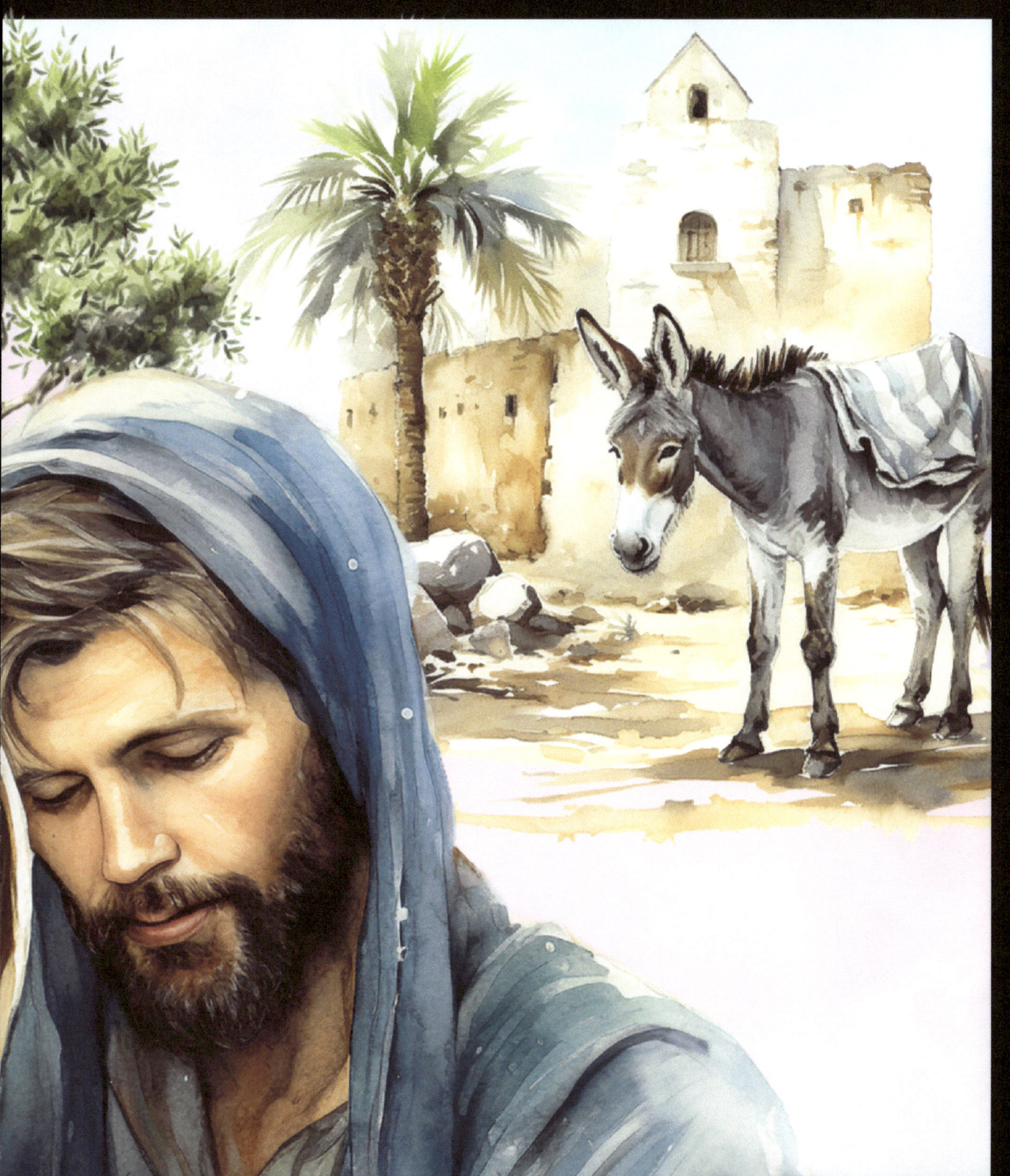

When Mary was pregnant, Caesar Augustus decreed that the world be taxed.

Joseph was of the lineage of King David; therefore, Joseph and Mary left Nazareth and went on a long journey to Bethlehem to be taxed.

This journey may have taken the couple about four days.

The city of Bethlehem must have been very crowded at that time because Mary and Joseph were unable to find a room at any inn. Therefore, they had to lodge in a stable where animals were kept.

While they were in the stable, Mary gave birth to baby Jesus. She wrapped him in swaddling cloths, which was the custom in those days. Then, she laid him in a manger that was used to feed larger farm animals.

Baby Jesus, who is also called the Lamb of God, was born in a stable.

One night, shepherds were watching over their sheep when suddenly, a bright light shone around them, and an angel appeared.

The angel told them that they should not be afraid because he was there to bring them the great news that a Savior had been born in Bethlehem. The angel also told them how to identify the baby. He would be dressed in swaddling clothes and would be lying in a manger. Many angels then joined that angel, and the host of angels glorified God.

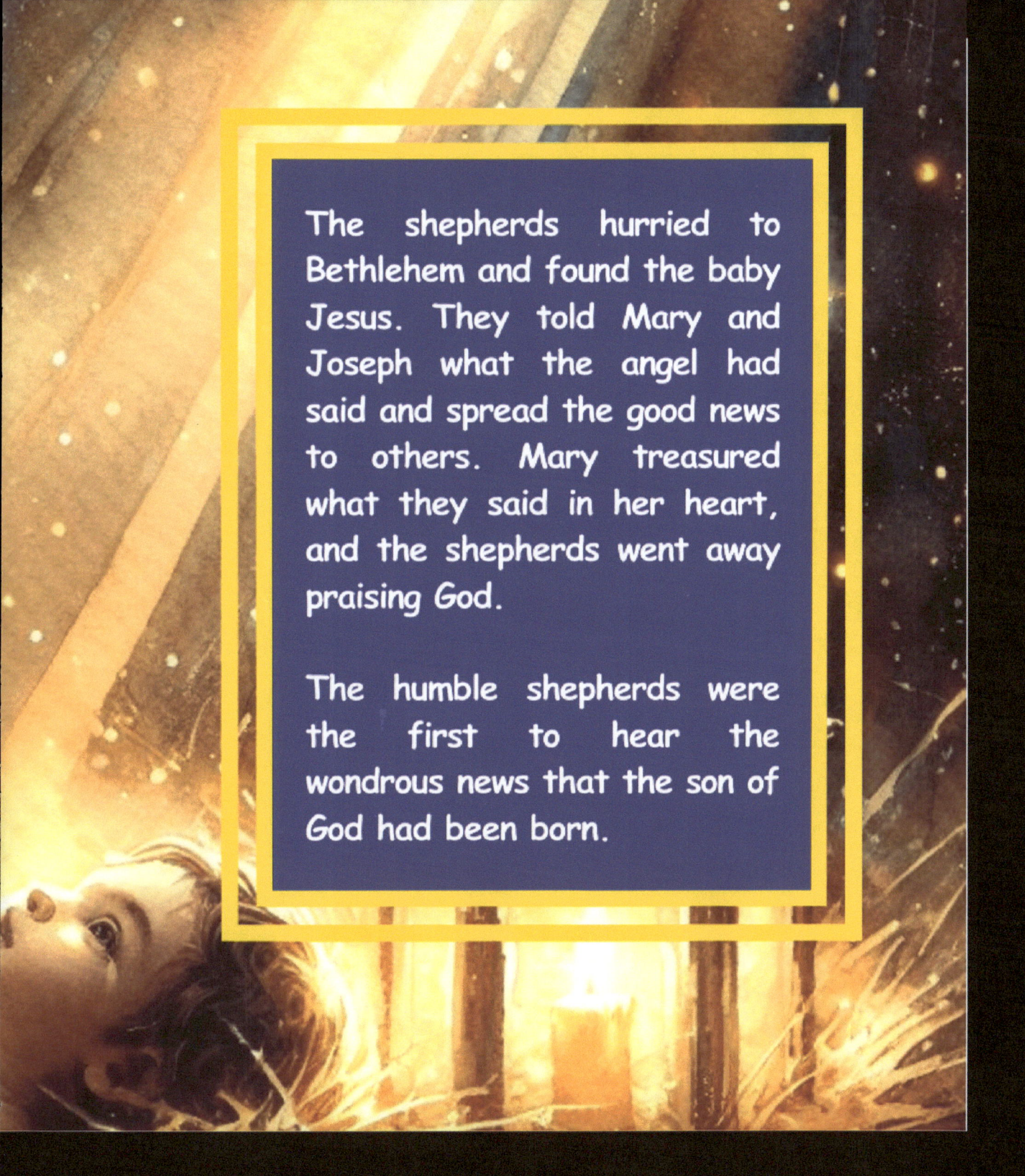

The shepherds hurried to Bethlehem and found the baby Jesus. They told Mary and Joseph what the angel had said and spread the good news to others. Mary treasured what they said in her heart, and the shepherds went away praising God.

The humble shepherds were the first to hear the wondrous news that the son of God had been born.

Wise men from a faraway land saw a star in the sky and knew that it was a sign that a king had been born.

When the wise men arrived at Jerusalem, they met King Herod, who was a cruel ruler.

When the King learned that the wise men were in search of a king who had been born, he felt threatened and afraid that this child might grow up and take his throne. Herod asked the wise men to continue to search for the child and bring him word as soon as they found him so that he could also worship the baby. However, King Herod really wanted to kill the baby.

The wise men left King Herod and continued to follow the star, which finally led them to where Jesus was. Jesus was a young child of about two years when the wise men found him.

When the wise men saw Jesus, they fell down and worshipped him and gave him gifts of gold, frankincense, and myrrh.

Later, they were warned in a dream not to return to Herod. They, therefore, decided to return to their country using a different path.

Mary and Joseph, a couple who were obedient to the will of God despite their humble beginnings in the city of Nazareth, were entrusted by God to bring up and care for the Savior of mankind. Together, they raised Jesus with a deep understanding of God's word.

The birth of Jesus Christ had been foretold many years before his birth. He was the anointed one who would defeat the devil. When Jesus grew up, he healed the sick, cast out devils from people, and raised others from the dead, just as the prophets said he would.

Our Heavenly Father wanted us to be reconciled to Him. He wanted to have a closer relationship with us, so he sent his Son into the world. When we accept Jesus into our hearts, our loving Heavenly Father gladly receives us.

"For God so loved the world, that he gave his only begotten Son, that whosoever believeth in him should not perish, but have everlasting life." John 3:16